First
Facts®

OUR GOVERNMENT

THE U.S. PRESIDENCY

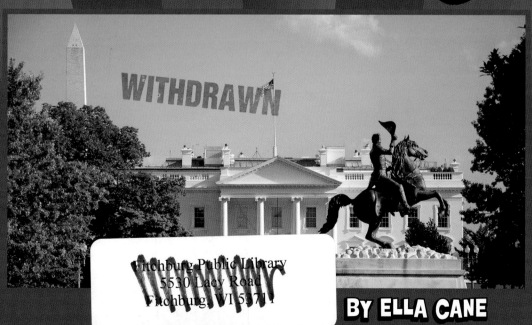

WITHDRAWN

BY ELLA CANE

CAPSTONE PRESS
a capstone imprint

First Facts are published by Capstone Press,
1710 Roe Crest Drive, North Mankato, Minnesota 56003
www.capstonepub.com

Library of Congress Cataloging-in-Publication Data
Cane, Ella.
The U.S. presidency / by Ella Cane.
     pages cm. — (First facts. our government)
Includes index.
Summary: "Informative, engaging text and vivid photos introduce readers
to the U.S. presidency"— Provided by publisher.
ISBN 978-1-4765-4200-3 (library binding)
ISBN 978-1-4765-5144-9 (paperback)
ISBN 978-1-4765-5997-1 (eBook PDF)
1. Presidents—United States—Juvenile literature. I. Title.
 JK517.C34 2014
  352.230973—dc23   2013028544

Editorial Credits
Shelly Lyons, editor; Kyle Grenz, designer; Wanda Winch, media researcher;
Eric Manske, production specialist

Photo Credits
AP Images: The White House/Eric Draper, cover (middle); Courtesy George W. Bush Library and
Museum, 7; Courtesy of the Ronald Reagan Library, cover (background), 17; Courtesy of the White
House: Pete Souza, 5, 21 (left); CriaImages.com: Jay Robert Nash Collection, 21 (right); Dreamstime:
Wangkun Jia, cover (Presidential Seal);

Library of Congress: Prints and Photographs Division, 9, Frances Benjamin Johnston, 15;
Shutterstock: Anatoly Tiplyashin, cover (top), Kamil Macniak, 11, Vacclav, 1; U.S. Marine Corps
photo: Lance Cpl. Ryan Rholes, 19

Printed in the United States of America in North Mankato, Minnesota.
122013   007914R

TABLE OF CONTENTS

LEADER OF THE UNITED STATES

Do you ever dream of being in charge? You could be, if you were the president of the United States!

The president is the leader of the country. He has one of the most important jobs in the nation's government. The president has many important duties.

WHO CAN BE PRESIDENT?

Being president is a tough job. Not everyone is able to have a chance at it. There are rules about who can run for president. The first rule is that you must be born in the United States or be born to U.S. **citizens**. Second, you must be at least 35 years old. Last, you must have lived in the United States for at least 14 years.

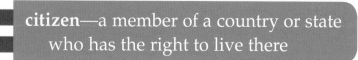

citizen—a member of a country or state who has the right to live there

CHAPTER 3

HOW WE ELECT A PRESIDENT

Every four years Americans vote for a president. Citizens must be 18 years old to vote. A president serves a **term** that lasts four years. Since 1947 a president is allowed to be **elected** for only two **consecutive** terms.

term—a set period of time
elect—to choose someone as leader by voting
consecutive—several in a row

FACT One president, Grover Cleveland, served two terms that were four years apart.

CHAPTER 4

THE PRESIDENT'S HOUSE

When a president takes office, he or she lives and works in the White House in Washington, D.C. The president's family lives there too. The West Wing of the White House is where the president and **staff** work. The president's office is called the Oval Office.

staff—a group of people who work for the same company or organization

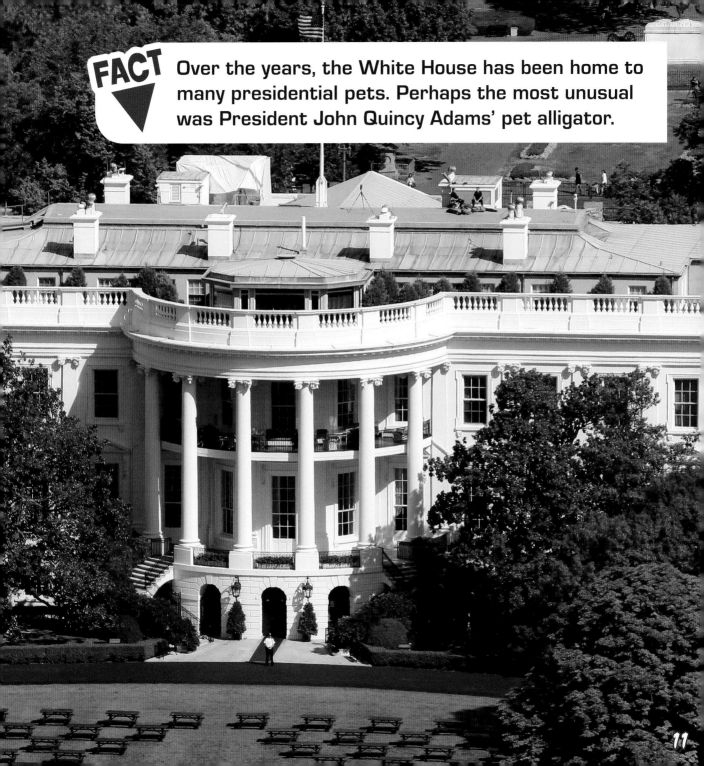

FACT Over the years, the White House has been home to many presidential pets. Perhaps the most unusual was President John Quincy Adams' pet alligator.

CHAPTER 5

PARTS OF THE U.S. GOVERNMENT

Three branches make up the U.S. government. The president is part of the executive branch, and he works with all three branches. The executive branch makes sure laws are followed. The legislative branch writes and passes the nation's laws. The judicial branch explains the U.S. **Constitution** and makes decisions on laws.

Constitution—the written system of laws in the United States; it states the rights of people and the powers of government

FEDERAL GOVERNMENT

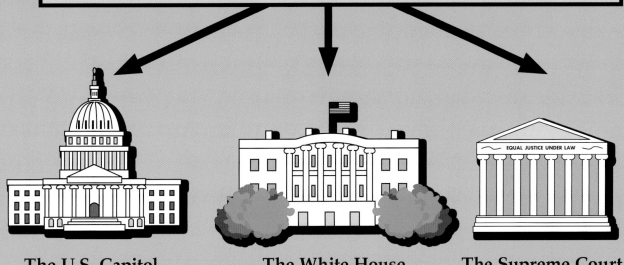

The U.S. Capitol

LEGISLATIVE

CONGRESS

SENATE

HOUSE OF
REPRESENTATIVES

The White House

EXECUTIVE

PRESIDENT

VICE
PRESIDENT

The Supreme Court

JUDICIAL

SUPREME
COURT

13

CHAPTER 6

THE PRESIDENT'S JOB

After being elected, it's time for the president to get to work. The president is head of the executive branch. He appoints, or chooses, 15 people to assist him. This group is called the president's **cabinet**. Cabinet members give the president suggestions about running the country. They also lead departments in the executive branch. For example, the Secretary of State leads the State Department.

FACT The president chooses cabinet members, but the legislative branch must approve them.

cabinet—a group of people who give suggestions to the president and lead government offices

President William McKinley (left) and his cabinet

The president works with the legislative branch. People in this branch pass **bills** to make laws. The president then approves or **vetoes** the bills.

The president also works with the judicial branch. He chooses the justices, or judges, for the **Supreme Court**. The people of the legislative branch then vote to approve the justices.

bill—a written idea for a new law
veto—the power of the president to keep a bill from being approved
Supreme Court—the most powerful court in the United States

FACT In 1981 President Ronald Reagan chose Sandra Day O'Connor as the first female Supreme Court Justice. She served 24 years on the Supreme Court.

Sandra Day O'Connor (right) being sworn in by Chief Justice Warren Burger (left). Her husband John O'Connor (middle) looks on.

The president is also the **commander in chief** of the United States armed forces. He can decide to send troops into battle.

In addition, the president is head of state. He represents the United States in other countries. The president often meets with leaders of other countries to keep good relations.

commander in chief—the leader of the armed forces

FACT The U.S. armed forces protect our country. They include the Army, Navy, Marines, Air Force, and Coast Guard.

CHAPTER 7

THE PRESIDENT'S DAY

The long list of duties leads to long workdays for the president. The president holds meetings, reads documents, and makes phone calls in the Oval Office. He meets with **Congress** and with leaders from other countries. Sometimes the president gives speeches. He also attends important events all over the world.

Congress—the elected group of people who make laws for the United States; Congress includes the House of Representatives and the Senate

Amazing but True!

Abraham Lincoln was the 16th president of the United States. As a young man, he had an interesting pastime—he was a wrestler! Lincoln lived in New Salem, Illinois, in 1831. A group of men from the town liked to challenge people to wrestling matches. The group's leader and Lincoln had several bouts, and Lincoln was the clear winner.

bill (BIL)—a written idea for a new law

cabinet (KA-buh-nit)—a group of people who give suggestions to the president and lead government offices

citizen (SIT-i-zuhn)—a member of a country or state who has the right to live there

commander in chief—(kuh-MAN-dur IN CHEEF) the leader of the armed forces

Congress (KON-gress)—the elected group of people who make laws for the United States; Congress includes the House of Representatives and the Senate

consecutive (kuhn-SEK-yuh-tiv)—several in a row

Constitution (kahn-stuh-TOO-shun)—the written system of laws in the United States; it states the rights of people and the power of government

elect (i-LEKT)—to choose someone as leader by voting

staff (STAF)—a group of people who work for the same company or organization

Supreme Court (suh-PREEM KORT)—the most powerful court in the United States

term (TURM)—a set period of time

veto (VEE-toh)—the power of the president to keep a bill from being approved

READ MORE

Cella, Clara. *President's Day*. Let's Celebrate. Mankato, Minn.: Capstone Press, 2013.

Grimes, Nikki. *Barack Obama: Son of Promise, Child of Hope*. New York: Little Simon, 2012.

Matzke, Ann H. *What Are the Branches of Democracy?* Little World Social Studies. Vero Beach, Fla.: Rourke Pub., 2012.

INTERNET SITES

FactHound offers a safe, fun way to find Internet sites related to this book. All of the sites on FactHound have been researched by our staff.

Here's all you do:

Visit *www.facthound.com*

Type in this code: 9781476542003

Super-cool stuff! Check out projects, games and lots more at
www.capstonekids.com

INDEX

CRITICAL THINKING USING THE COMMON CORE

1. A person can be elected president for only two terms. This was not always the case. Use Internet and printed sources to find out when and why this law was passed. Tell whether you agree or disagree, supporting your answer with sources. (Integration of Knowledge and Ideas)
2. Congress has the power to approve or reject the president's choices for Supreme Court justices. What are some of the reasons why Congress has that power? (Key Ideas and Details)